Usborne
First Numbers

Jo Litchfield and Felicity Brooks

Photography by Howard Allman

Mathematics consultant: Frances Mosley

Managing designer: Mary Cartwright

With thanks to Staedtler for providing
the Fimo® material for models

A note for parents and teachers

Even before they can read, many young children enjoy counting and can often recognize numbers. This book has been carefully designed to help both readers and pre-readers develop these vital number skills in a fun way. Try talking about the pictures with your child, count the objects with them and help them read the text and solve the "puzzles". Also try to encourage them to use number skills such as counting, sequencing and addition in everyday situations at home and in the classroom.

Each double-page spread of this book is self-contained, so you can look at the pages in any order, though the easier tasks are nearer the beginning. At the back is an explanation of the symbols used and a glossary to help with the meanings of new words.

Here are some of the people you will meet in this book:

Sally   Olivia   Ethan   Pete   Suzie   Minnie and her dad

Contents

Aggie and
her babies   Paolo   Jenny   Billy   Danny   Charlie

Counting to 10

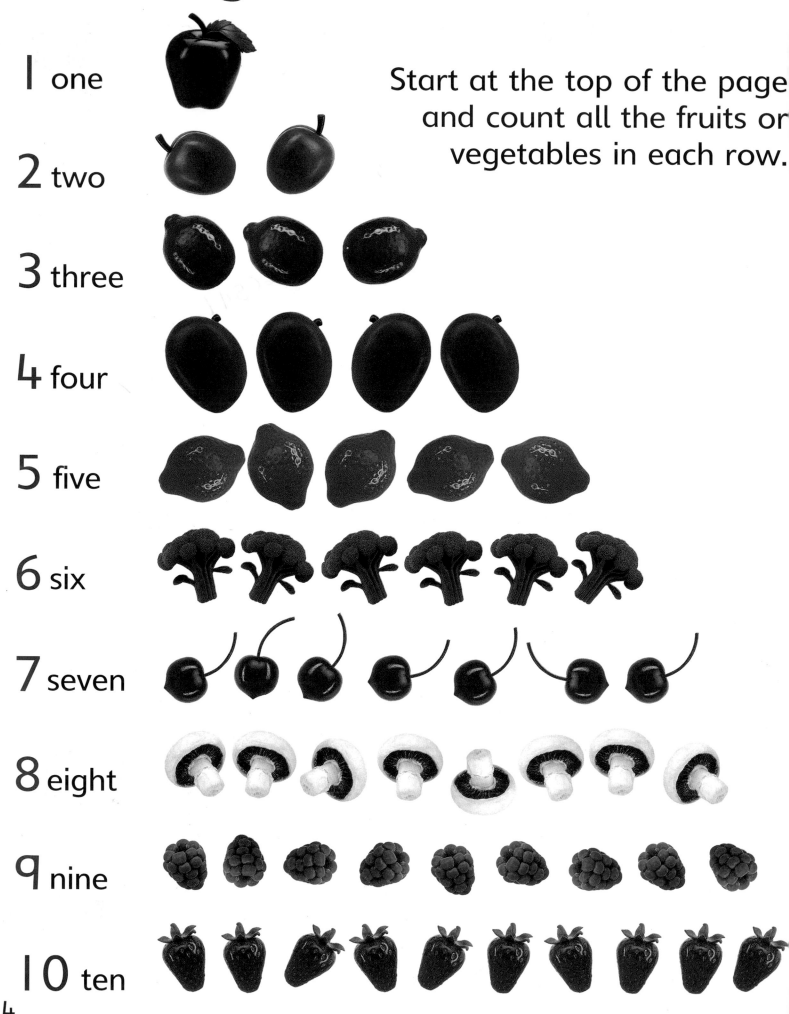

Start at the top of the page and count all the fruits or vegetables in each row.

1 one

2 two

3 three

4 four

5 five

6 six

7 seven

8 eight

9 nine

10 ten

Counting on the farm

Can you spot all these things on the farm?

 4 turkeys

3 sheep

 2 cows

 7 geese

1 farmer

 4 ducklings

 6 ducks

 8 hens

 5 chicks

What else can you see?

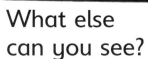

5

Counting down

Count the animals in each row.

10 ten
9 nine
8 eight
7 seven
6 six
5 five
4 four
3 three
2 two
1 one

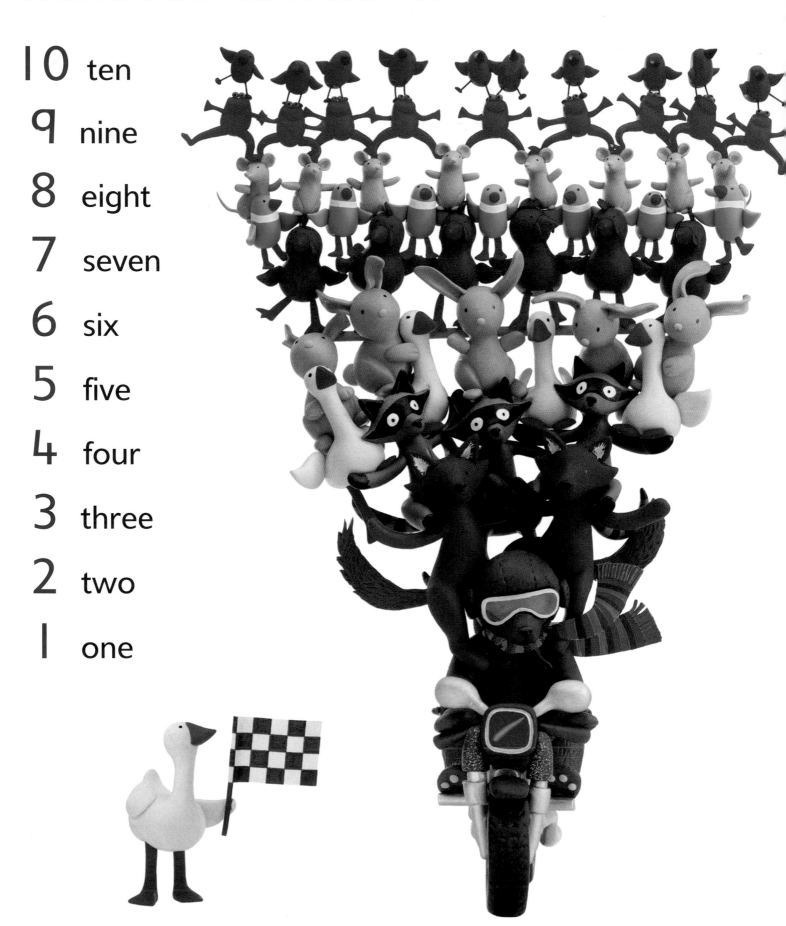

Can you count to 20?

1 one
2 two
3 three
4 four
5 five
6 six
7 seven
8 eight
9 nine
10 ten
11 eleven
12 twelve
13 thirteen
14 fourteen
15 fifteen
16 sixteen
17 seventeen
18 eighteen
19 nineteen
20 twenty

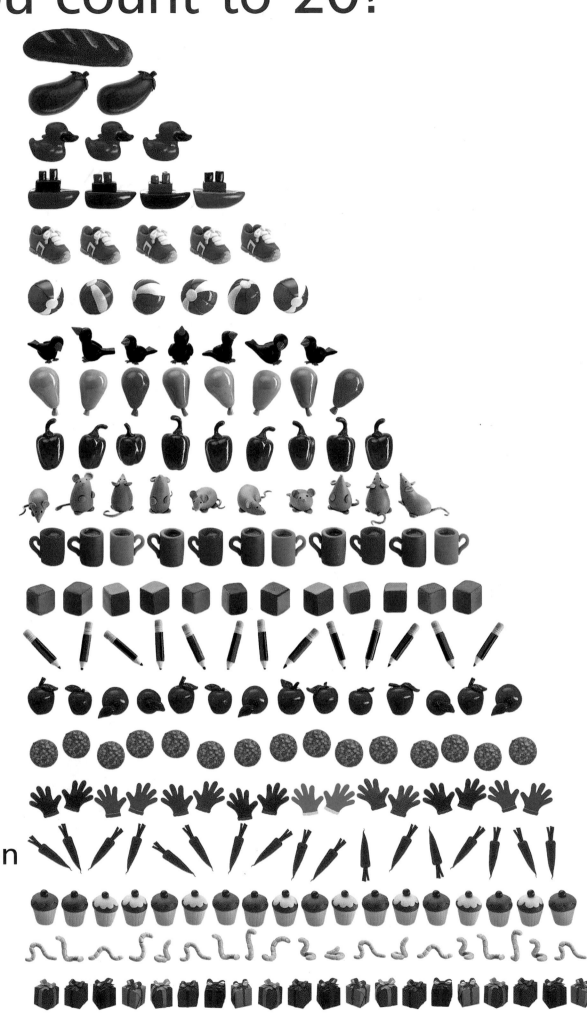

In the classroom

Can you help these children arrange their classroom?

Space for 6 coats

Blue books

Yellow books

Blue paint

Red paint

Yellow paint

16 pieces

Where can Molly hang up her coat?

Where could these 2 bottles of paint fit?

Where could this block fit?

Where does this crayon belong?

Is there space for another child in the playhouse?

Only 2 children at a time

Reading corner

Green books

Where could this green book go?

Is there space for Suzie in the reading corner?

9

Numbers in the town

Can you spot all these numbers?

1 2 3 4 5 6 7 8 9 10

Which table are Suzie and her daddy sitting at?

How long will it be until the next bus arrives?

How long will it be until the hairdresser returns?

How many parking spaces are left?

When will the postman collect Jack's letter?

What comes next?

Ben   Joshua   Olivia   Ethan   Freya   Annie   Paolo

How old do you think Paolo is?

0 1 2 3 4 5 6 7 8 9 10 11 12 13 14

Where do you think Suzie will land next?

Greta   Naomi   Helen   Jo   Zoe

What size T-shirt do you think Greta needs?

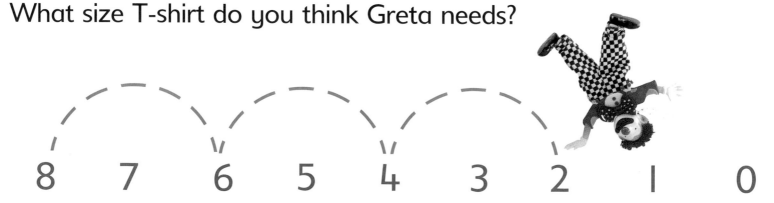

8 7 6 5 4 3 2 1 0

Where do you think Charlie will land next?

Find the missing number

What's the number on the very muddy girl's shirt?

What number should the blue hut have?

What do you think is the number of the cake that won?

What number was on Greta's balloon?

Odd numbers, even numbers

1 2 3 4 5 6 7 8 9 10 11 12 13 14 15

This blue bunny only jumps on odd numbers. Where do you think it will land next?

1 2 3 4 5 6 7 8 9 10 11 12 13 14 15

This pink bunny only jumps on even numbers. Where do you think it will land next?

Who are wearing odd numbers, the boys or girls?
Who are wearing even numbers?

Now who are wearing the odd numbers?
Now who are wearing the even numbers?

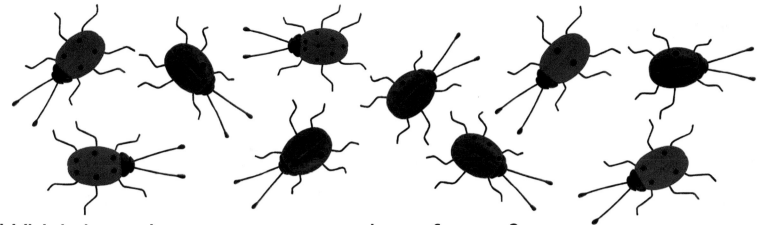

Which bugs have an even number of spots?
Which bugs have an odd number of spots?

These teddy bears are about
to play soccer. The odds are
going to play the evens, but
they are all mixed up.

Point to the bears wearing the odd numbers.
Now point to the bears wearing the even numbers.

More or fewer?

Jessie

Dina

Billy   Sally

Jessie has more puppies than Dina.

Who has more toy cars?

The orange cat has fewer cushions to sit on.

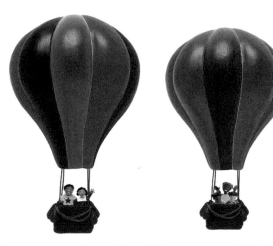

Point to the balloon which has fewer people in its basket.

Which of these two lines has more people in it?

Which cake has more candles?   Which hen has fewer chicks?

More or less?

Danny   Millie

Millie has more juice than Danny.

Ethan   Olivia

Ethan has less ice cream than Olivia.

Sarah   Pete

Who has less bread, Sarah or Pete?

Amy   Sally

Who has more sand, Amy or Sally?

Which of these sandcastles has more sand in it?

Most and fewest

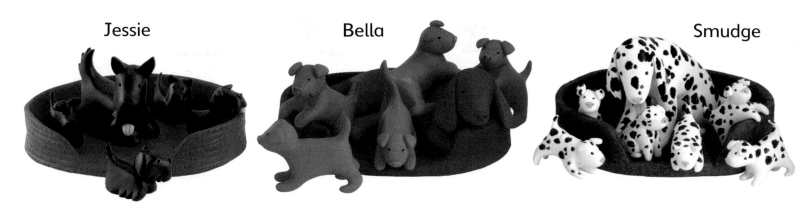

Jessie   Bella   Smudge

Who has the most puppies, Jessie, Bella or Smudge?

Which caterpillar has the most black stripes?

Aggie   Tim   Janet   Nick

Who is taking care of the fewest children?

Which duck has the fewest ducklings?

Most and least

Which sandcastle has the least sand in it?

Which bathtub has the most foam?

Who is buying the most food? Who is buying the least?

One more

Look carefully at this picture.

Where could you hang one more saucepan?

Where could you hang one more spoon?

Who needs to add one more spoonful of cake mixture?

Who do you think needs one more block?

Who needs one more jigsaw puzzle piece?

Which puzzle needs one more shape?

 Where is there space for one more game?

 Which box has space for one more crayon?

Which box has space for one more bottle of paint?

21

How many more?

Mr. Bun the baker has been busy in the kitchen, but he still has a few things to do.

How many more gingerbread men does he need to fill the tray?

How many more spoonfuls of muffin mix does he need to fill the tray?

How many more loaf tins does he still need to fill?

How many more loaves does he need to fill the red box?

How many more bagels are needed to fill the boxes?

How many more cupcakes still need cherries?

How many more children need swimming goggles?

How many more acrobats are needed to make a pyramid?

Each monkey wants a banana. How many more do they need?

How many more cars can fit here?

How many more workers need hard hats?

Adding together

2 children are playing here.

2 more children join them.

Now there are 4 children.

Two children and two children make four children all together. In numbers, you can write this:

$$2 + 2 = 4$$

There are 2 girls at Ellie's party.

3 more of her friends arrive.

Now how many children are there?

$$2 + 3 = ?^5$$

There are 3 frogs on a lily pad.

3 more frogs swim over to join them.

How many frogs are there now?

$$3 + 3 = ?\ 6$$

Try some more adding.

Jenny's train only has 1 wagon.	Ethan brings her 4 more.	How many wagons are there now?

1   +   4   =   5

There are 2 bees on this flower.	4 more bees fly down to join them.	How many bees are there now?

2   +   4   =   ? 6

Becky only has 2 strawberries.	Auntie Ally gives her 5 more.	How many does she have now?

2   +   5   =   7

More adding together

There are 5 kittens in the basket.

Tabby brings 3 more kittens.

How many kittens are there now?

5   +   3   =   8

There are 6 sunflowers in this wheelbarrow.

Aggie puts 3 more flowers in the wheelbarrow.

How many sunflowers are there all together?

6   +   3   =   9

Billy has used 8 bricks so far.

He adds 2 more to the pile.

Now how many bricks has he used?

8   +   2   =   10

Playing shopping

These children have made a little shop and some pretend money. They call their money "plobs".

This is what plobs look like.

Jack has 5 plobs. Suzie has 10 plobs. If they put their money together, could they buy the car?

Ethan and Pete have 2 plobs each. What can they buy if they put their money together?

Danny has two 5 plob coins. Does he have enough to buy the robot?

Olivia has a 10 plob coin and two 2 plob coins. What could she buy?

9 plobs

14 plobs

10 for 5 plobs

6 plobs

4 plobs

15 plobs

Which is the cheapest toy? Which is the most expensive?

If you had two 10 plob coins, what would you buy?

Making 10

Tina is setting the table for 10 friends, but she's missing a few things.

How many more plates does she need?

$8 + ? = 10$
2

How many more forks does she need?

$5 + 5 = 10$

How many more cups does she need?

$4 + 6 = 10$

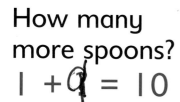

How many more spoons?

$1 + 9 = 10$

How many more place-mats?

$3 + 7 = 10$

How many more knives?

$6 + 4 = 10$

Mrs. Martin likes to have 10 of everything on display at her fruit stall.

How many more oranges does she need?

 How many more pears?

How many more lemons?

How many more peaches?

There are 10 seats here. How many more people can sit down?

3
7
5
5
6

Each pair of numbers adds up to 10. What's the hidden number?

One less

Oliver Muncher has 7 apples.

He eats one of his apples.

Now he has 6. He has one less.

Seven apples take away one apple leaves six apples. In numbers, you can write this:

$$7 - 1 = 6$$

Dina the dog has 3 puppies.

One puppy goes to play.

How many puppies are left in the basket?

$$3 - 1 = 2$$

5 little birds are eating seeds.

One of the birds flies away.

How many birds are there now?

$$5 - 1 = \ ?$$

Patch looks very interested in all this party food.

A little later the children come in. Look at the two pictures carefully. Can you see what Patch has eaten?

How many are left?

The farm is full of animals. Can you spot them all?

Can you
see 1 cat?

Count 2
cows.

Find 3
goats.

Spot 4
turkeys.

Spot 5
sheep.

Find 6
ducks.

Spot 7
hens.

Spot 8
chicks.

Now some of the animals have gone into the barn.

The cat has gone in. How many cats are left?
1 – 1 = ?

4 hens have gone in. How many are left?
7 – 4 = ?

1 goat has gone in. How many are left?
3 – 1 = ?

1 cow has gone in. How many are left?
2 – 1 = ?

2 sheep have gone in.
5 – 2 = ?

2 turkeys have gone in.
4 – 2 = ?

3 ducks have gone in.
6 – 3 = ?

4 chicks have gone in.
8 – 4 = ?

Taking away

Charlie is juggling with 5 balls.	He drops 2 of the balls.	Now he juggles with 3 balls.
5	– 2 =	3

There are 3 cats on the sofa.	One of the cats jumps off.	How many cats are left?
3	– 1 =	?

There are 6 dog biscuits.	Smudge eats 2 of them.	How many dog biscuits are left?
6	– 2 =	?

There are 4 teddy bears in the bed.	Harry and Sophie take 2 away.	How many teddy bears are left?

$$4 \qquad - \qquad 2 \qquad = \qquad ?$$

There are 7 crows on the scarecrow.	4 of the crows fly away.	How many crows are left?

$$7 \qquad - \qquad 4 \qquad = \qquad ?$$

There are 8 cup-cakes on this plate.	Oliver Muncher eats 3 of them.	How many cup-cakes are left?

$$8 \qquad - \qquad 3 \qquad = \qquad ?$$

Matching and sorting

Can you find where everything should go in this messy bedroom?

Where do tapes go?

Find the shoe that goes with this one.

Find this toy cow. Where do you think it should go?

This hat is on the bed, but where should it be ?

 Can you find this toy giraffe? Where should it go?

 Can you see 3 toy cars? Where should they go?

 Find the sock that matches this one.

Find this drum. Where should it go?

How many playing cards can you find?

Hats

Musical instruments

Find 3 CDs and the box where they go.

Which glove goes with this one?

Multiplying by 2

Here are 2 tiger cubs.

Each tiger cub has 2 ears.

The 2 cubs have 4 ears all together.

Another way to say this is "two groups of two is four" or "two times two is four". In numbers you write this

$$2 \times 2 = 4$$

Here are 3 alarm clocks.

Each alarm clock has 2 bells.

How many bells all together?

$$3 \times 2 = ?$$

Here are 4 children.

Each child has 2 hands.

How many hands all together?

$$4 \times 2 = ?$$

Can you help these children finish making their potato people?

Olivia has 1 person. How many arms does she need?
1 x 2 = ?

Suzie has 2 people. How many mouths does she need?
2 x 1 = ?

Ethan has 3 potato people. How many ears does he need?
3 x 2 = ?

Sally has 4 people. How many ears does she need?
4 x 2 = ?

Billy has 6 people. How many eyes does he need?
6 x 2 = ?

Jenny has 7 potato people. How many feet does she need?
7 x 2 = ?

Feet   Mouths   Arms   Ears   Eyes

Multiplying by 10

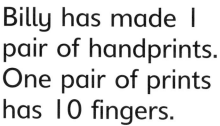   

Billy has made 1 pair of handprints. One pair of prints has 10 fingers.
1 x 10 = 10

Billy and Suzie have made 2 pairs of prints. How many fingers all together?
2 x 10 = ?

Billy, Suzie and Pete have made 3 pairs of prints. How many fingers all together?
3 x 10 = ?

A monster left these footprints. Each print has 10 toes. How many toe prints all together?
5 x 10 = ?

How many sheep are there here? How many legs do the sheep have all together?
10 x 4 =?

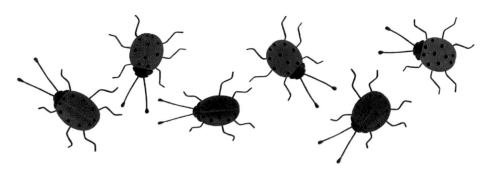

Each of these beetles has 10 spots.
How many spots are there all together?

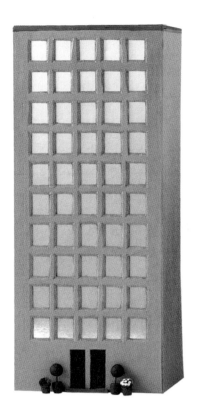

Each flower has 10 petals.
How many petals all together?

This building has 10 floors.
How many windows can
you see all together?

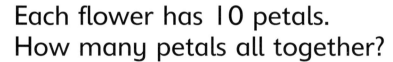

Each of these giraffes has 10 spots.
How many spots are there all together?

How many noses do these 10 children have all together?
How many feet? How many toes?

Double trouble

How many children are there here?

How many are there on the slide?
How many are there on the seesaw?

Now all their twins have joined in. How many children are on the slide now? How many are on the seesaw?

Half a bagel

Each mouse has half a bagel.

Pete has drunk half of his juice.

Minnie is half the height of her dad.

Sally has eaten half of her pizza. How much does she have left?

Half of Pip's buttons are red and half are yellow. How many are red?

Bill and Ben are sharing 8 cherries. How many does each one get?

Half of these girls like football. How many is that?

43

Counting to 100

Here are 100 caterpillars.

1 2 3 4 5

6 7 8 9 10

11 12 13 14 15

16 17 18 19 20

21 22 23 24 25

26 27 28 29 30

31 32 33 34 35

36 37 38 39 40

41 42 43 44 45

46 47 48 49 50

Can you find out how many caterpillars there are on each page without counting them all?

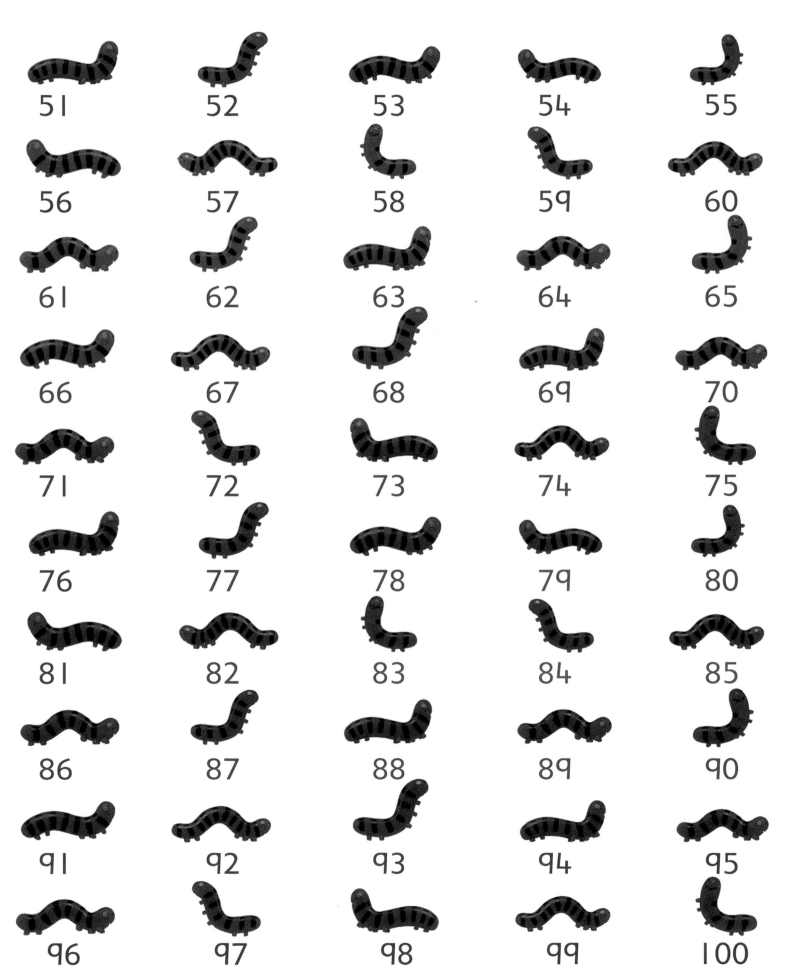

51 52 53 54 55

56 57 58 59 60

61 62 63 64 65

66 67 68 69 70

71 72 73 74 75

76 77 78 79 80

81 82 83 84 85

86 87 88 89 90

91 92 93 94 95

96 97 98 99 100

1,000 ducks?

How many ducks are there in a square?
Do all the squares have the same number of ducks?